This
Bible Story Time
book belongs to

_____

_____

_____

For Lucy – E.C.

Text by Sophie Piper
Illustrations copyright © 2006 Estelle Corke
This edition copyright © 2006 Lion Hudson

The moral rights of the author and illustrator
have been asserted

A Lion Children's Book
an imprint of
Lion Hudson plc
Mayfield House, 256 Banbury Road,
Oxford OX2 7DH, England
www.lionhudson.com
ISBN-13 978 0 7459 4871 3
ISBN-10 0 7459 4871 5

First edition 2006
1 3 5 7 9 10 8 6 4 2 0

All rights reserved

The Lord's Prayer (on page 10) from Common Worship: Services and
Prayers for the Church of England (Church House Publishing, 2000)
is copyright © The English Language Liturgical Consultation, 1988.

A catalogue record for this book is available
from the British Library

Typeset in 20/24 Baskerville MT Schlbk
Printed and bound in China

BIBLE STORY TIME

Jesus and the Prayer

Sophie Piper * Estelle Corke

LION
CHILDREN'S

One day, Jesus saw that crowds had come to see him.

He went to the top of a hill near Lake Galilee. Everyone sat down to listen.

'Are you here because you want to be God's friend?' he asked. 'If you are, you can feel truly happy.

'God welcomes you into the kingdom of heaven!

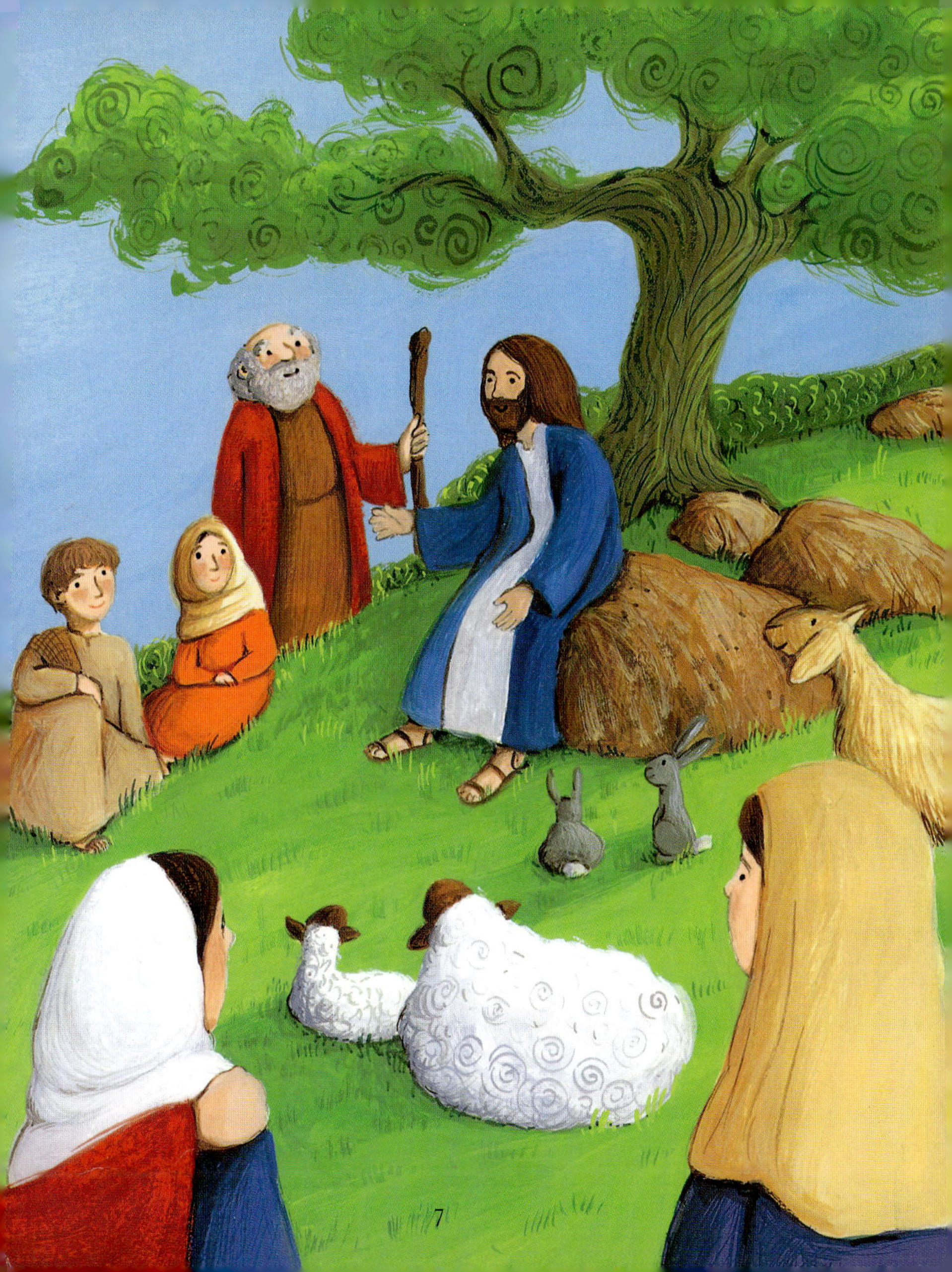

'God's friends should always want to do good – even to people they don't like.

'Even to people who are cruel to them.

'The Roman soldiers are allowed to ask us to carry their heavy packs for one whole mile.

'When that happens, offer to carry it for two miles.

'Take time alone to pray to God. Say this:

*'Our Father in heaven,
hallowed be your name,
your kingdom come,
your will be done,
on earth as in heaven.
Give us today our daily bread.
Forgive us our sins
as we forgive those who sin against us.
Lead us not into temptation
but deliver us from evil.'*

'You must always forgive people, even if they have been very bad to you. Then you can be sure that God will forgive you.

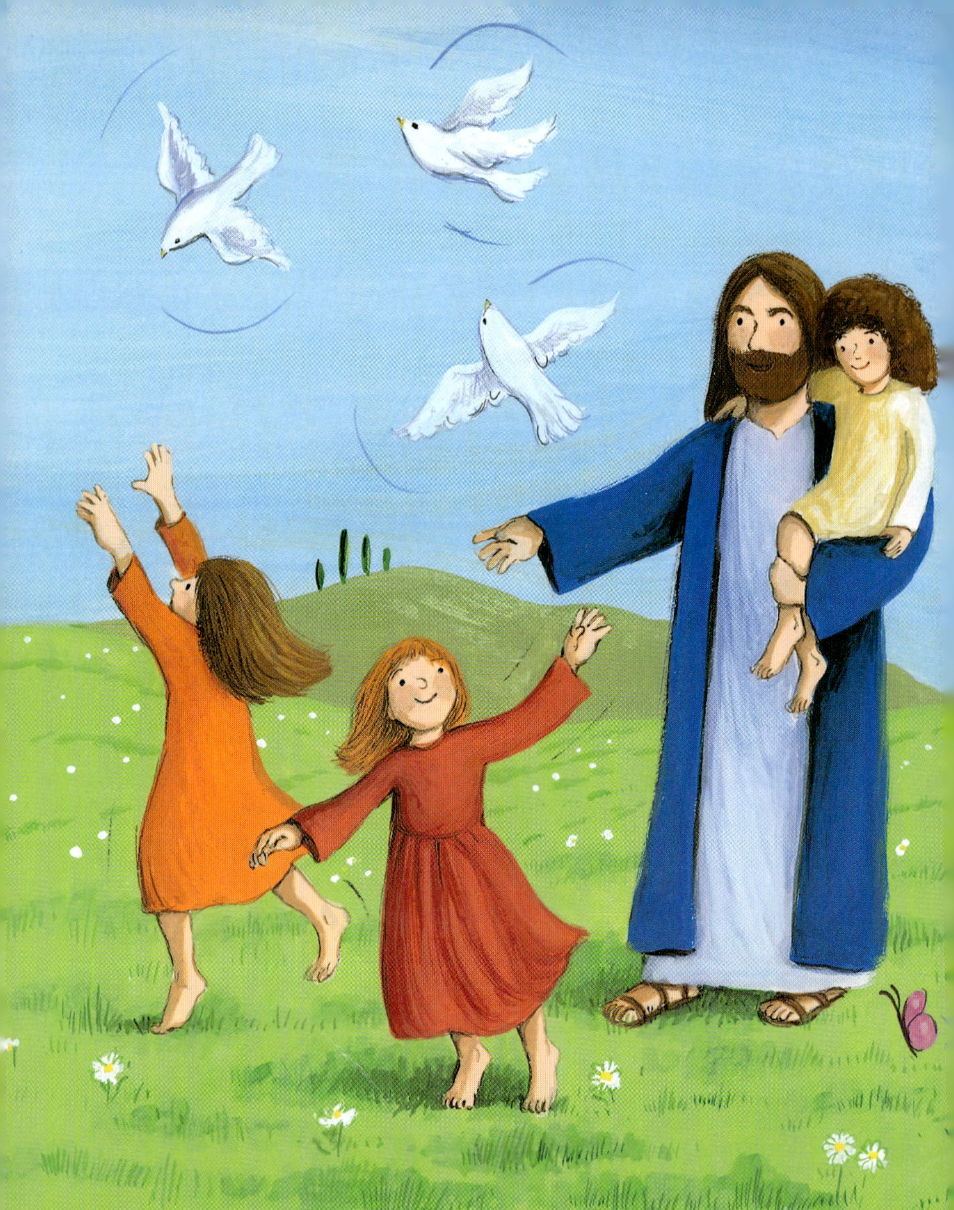

'Don't waste your time trying to be rich. God will make sure you have all you need.

'Look at the birds. They don't sow seeds or gather a harvest.

'Even so, God takes care of them.

'Look at the flowers. They don't spend their time weaving and sewing.

'Even so, the petals they wear are lovelier than the finest clothes.

'God cares about petals that last a day. God cares even more about you.

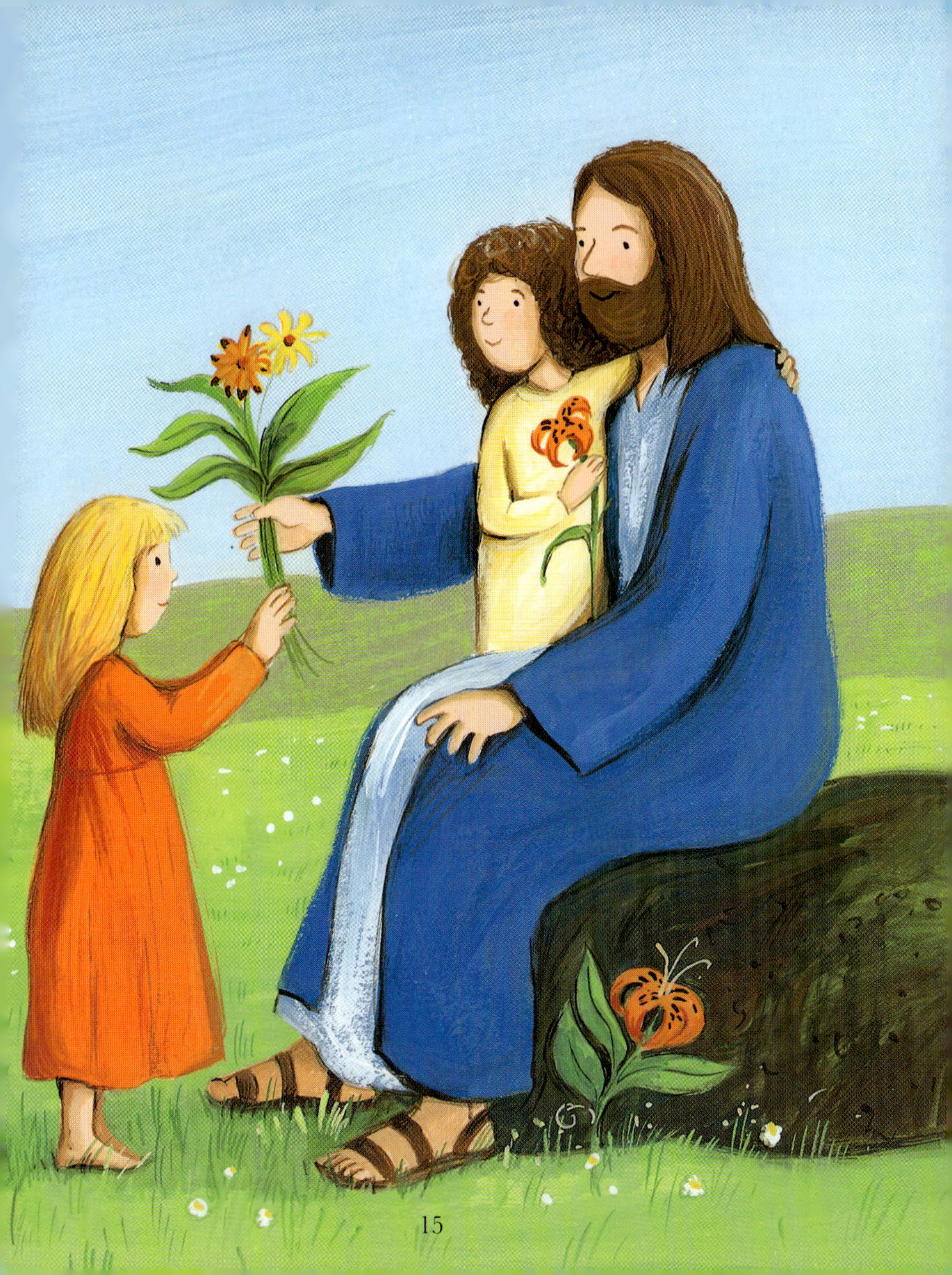

'I can see you all listening, and that is good.

'You must also do what I say.

'I will tell you a story. It is about two men who each wanted to build a house.

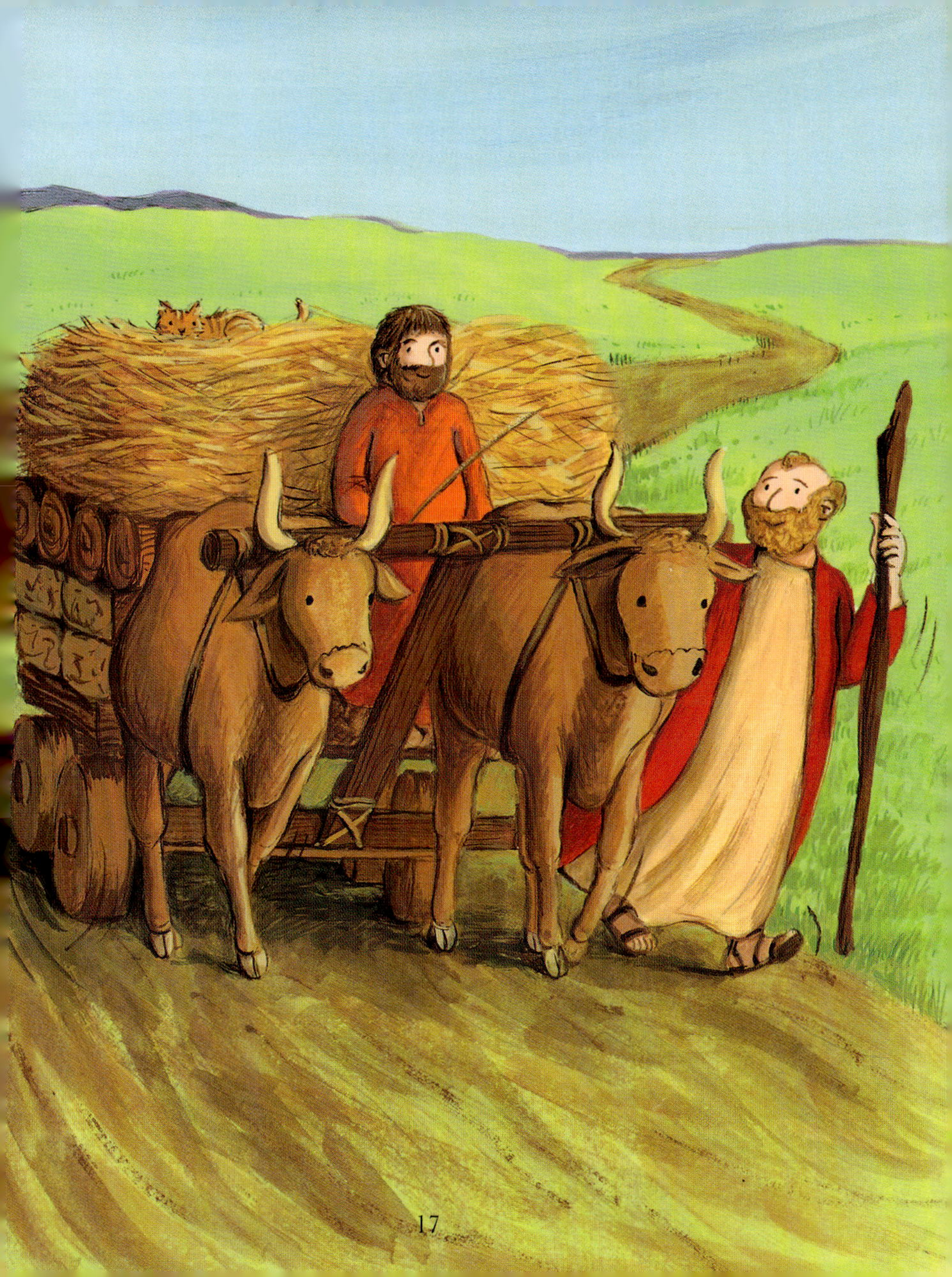

' "I want my house now," said one. "This sandy soil down by the river is easy to dig.

' "I won't have to carry my building things far."

'His house was ready in no time. He had a lovely, lazy summer.

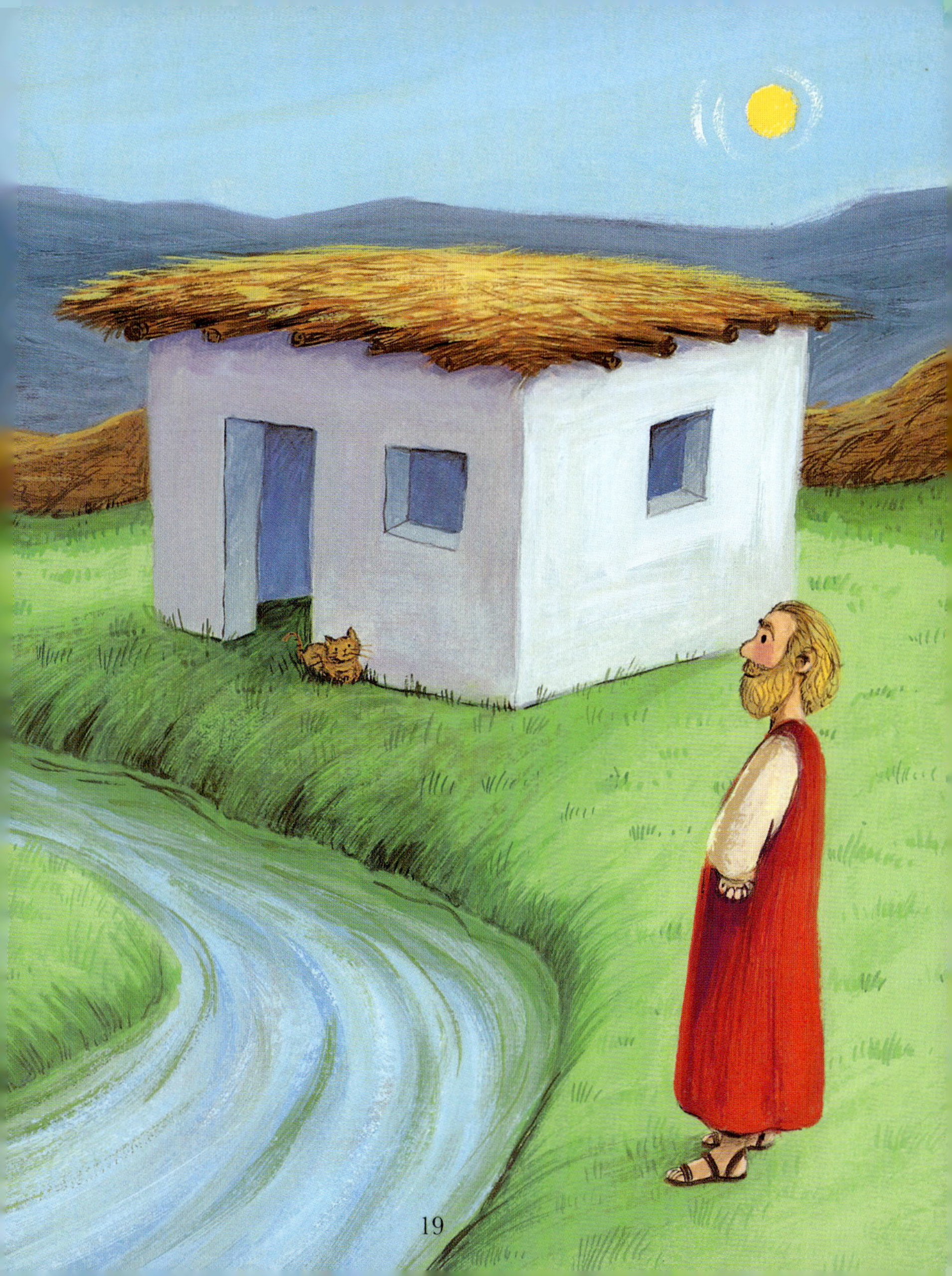

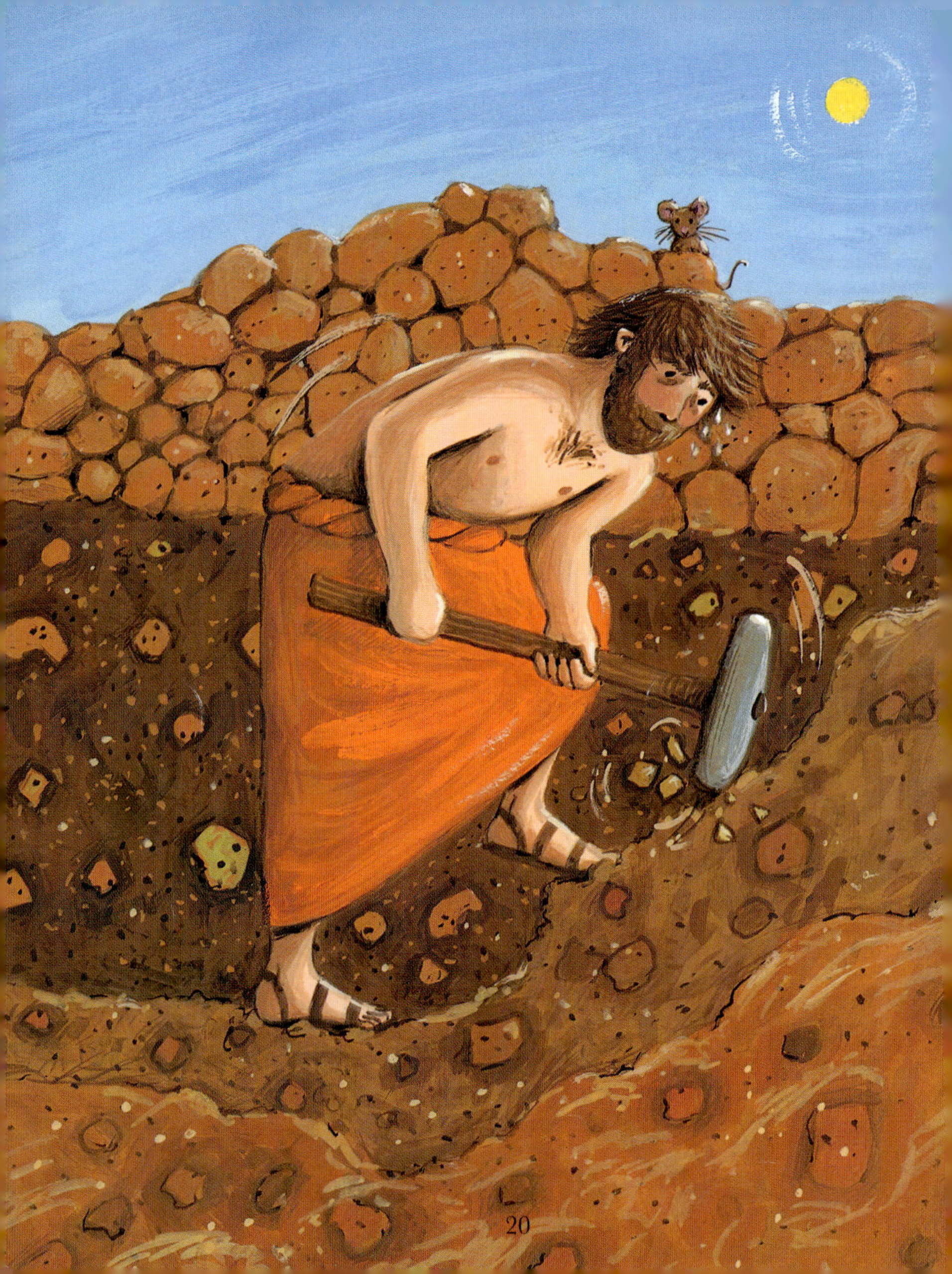

' "I want my house to last," said the other.

' "I will build my house up here on the rock."

'It was hard work. He had to chip out the foundations with a hammer.

'He had to carry his building things up high.

'By the time he had finished, the summer had gone.

'Then came winter: the wind blew cold, the rain hissed down.

'The river rose higher and higher.
'It overflowed its banks.
'Soon it was lapping around the house on the sandy soil.

'Suddenly a wave came tumbling down the river. It swept the house away.

'"Oh, how foolish I was," cried the man.

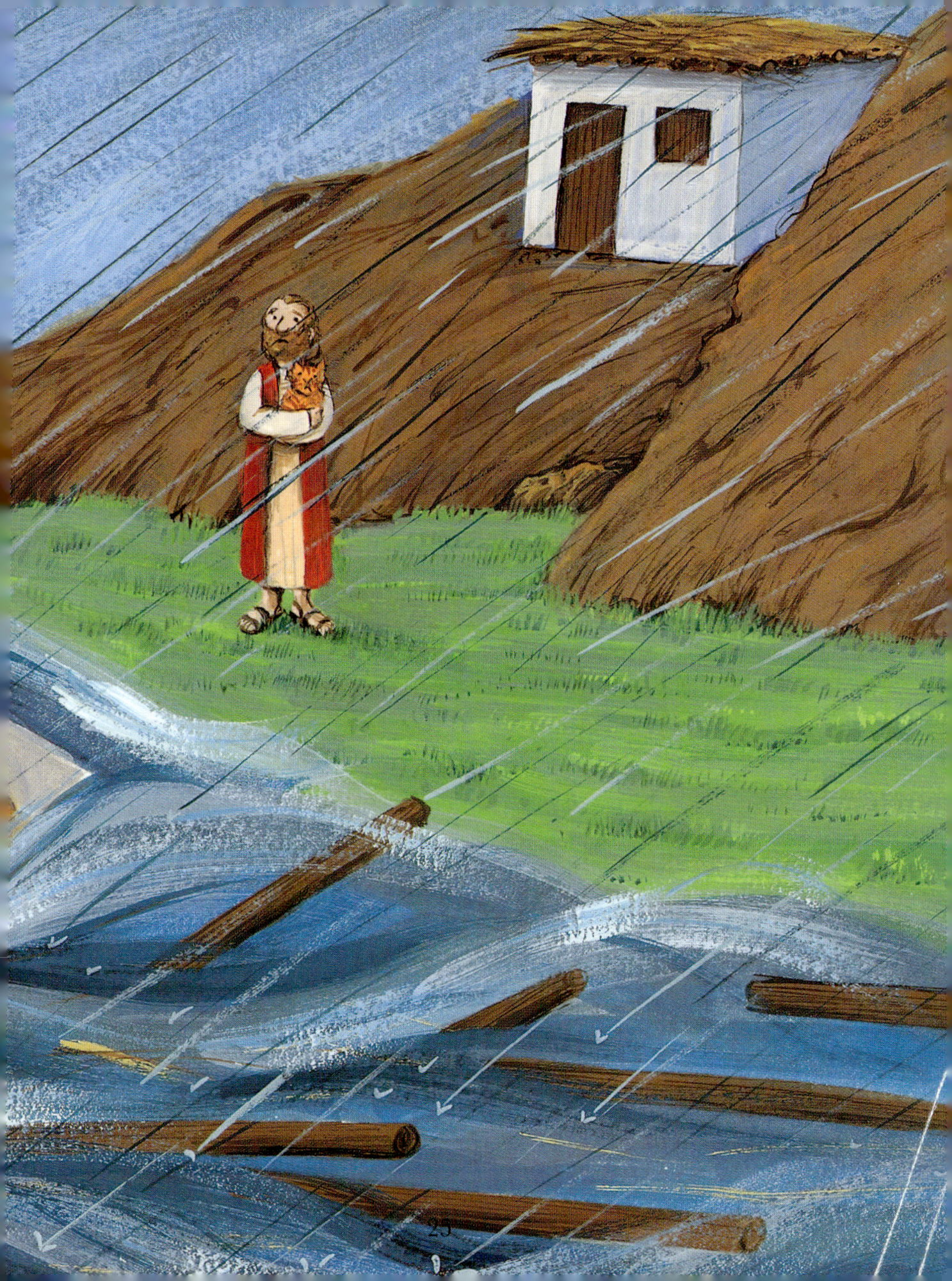

'Up on the rock, the other man nodded sadly.

' "I think I made the wise choice," he said. "My house is safe. It is truly going to last. The storms will not reach it." '

Jesus looked at the crowds. 'If you listen to what I say and then forget it, you are like the foolish man.

'If you listen to what I say and obey it, you are like the wise man.

'You will do wonderful things with your life, and God will bless you.'